Bland Irish Food

Copyright Text & Illustration
© 2015 S.H. Ryan
All rights reserved.
ISBN-13: 978-1517417444

A Celebration of Irish 'Cuisine'

Why not celebrate Irish food? Well, there are many reasons why not, from our lack of any kind of fancy spices to the fact that we like to eat the same thing again and again and again. The Irish are undoubtedly the fastest eaters on the planet, partly because our taste buds are so underdeveloped and partly because we've more important things to be doing.

You also have to remember that the food stuff that best represents the Irish to the world, the potato, killed a quarter of us back in the good oul days, so no wonder we're not too enthusiastic about food.

And so to celebrate all that's goopy about Irish cuisine, here is a selection of our most beloved dishes, or at least the stuff that sat in our bellies while we were running up and down the streets or in the fields, wearing T-shirts in November. And if you have any queries or concerns, don't hesitate to reflect on them.

Table of Contents

Hearth & Home 6

Bacon, Cabbage, and Spuds 7

Colcannon 9

Irish Stew 11

Roast Chicken 13

Coddle 15

Read This 18

Lasagna 19

Vegetarian Lasagna 21

Boxty 22

Roast Beef Dinner 24

Black Pudding 26

Sundries 29

Sugary Toast 30

Irish Scones 32

Egg in a Cup 34

See This 36

Crisp Sandwich 37

Summer Salad (aka Winter Salad) 39

Soda Bread 41

Desserts 43

Sherry Trifle 44

Agree With This 47

Queen Cakes/Fairy Cakes 48

Barmbrack 52

Christmas Pudding 55

Think About This 58

Christmas Cake 60

Neapolitan Ice Cream Wafers 64

The Drink 65

A Nice Cup of Tea, Just a Half for Me 67

Coffee Made on Milk 69

Irish Coffee 70

Stay Away From This 71

Poitín 72

Minerals 72

Irish Whiskey 73

Your Notes 75

Hearth & Home

Bacon, Cabbage, and Spuds

If there is a contender for the national dish of Ireland, then bacon with cabbage and potatoes is high on the list. Surveys carried over the years asking people what they traditionally eat on St. Patrick's Day have often come up with the result 'pints,' but when asked what they _would like_ to eat on this festive day, the bacon dish has always been a winner.

This dish includes all the major food groups: meat, vegetables, potatoes, and dairy (in the liberal amount of butter used). It has built generations of overly fertile women and fine, hardy men who don't fall down when you punch them the first time (and then you better run).

Who needs gravy?

Ingredients:

- A good-looking joint of bacon;
- A good head of cabbage;
- A good few spuds (about 30), no 'mowldy' smell.
-

Method:

1. Place bacon joint in a pot of cold water. Remove from the water and take off the plastic wrapper. Return to water.
2. Bring to the boil, then cover and simmer for 30 minutes per pound.
3. Remove the scum that floats to the top of the water if it makes you feel better.
4. Meanwhile, clean the insects off the cabbage and give it a good chop. Place the cabbage pieces into another pot of water, and boil for about 20 minutes. Don't go mad with the boiling as you want to keep some texture and some taste. And vitamins.
5. Get another bloody pot and add the peeled potatoes to that one. Boil away to your heart's content. See next recipe if you want to make colcannon.
6. Eat away, have babies, and fight.

Colcannon

Colcannon is a fine dish, so don't say anything bad about it or you'll get a box.

The name comes from 'cál ceannann,' meaning 'white-speckled cabbage.' The best colcannon dishes involve summoning the god of potatoes, Poitín, to infuse the potatoes with a nice potatoey flavor. If that doesn't work, a full pound of butter and a carton of full-fat cream should do the trick.

Colcannon – Good for lining the stomach and the arteries.

Ingredients:

- 500g potatoes;
- 100g cabbage or curly kale (whatever that is);
- 250g scallions (spring onions to the heathens);
- A butter factory.

Method:

1. Boil the bejeesus out of the potatoes and mash them like the divil.
2. Finely chop the cabbage/kale and the scallions.
3. Mash the spuds and the green stuff together and then blend in as much full-fat, salty butter as you can.
4. Serve with boiled ham (did I mention that you have to make that as well? So in effect, you should have started this recipe two hours ago).

Difficulty level: Medium (you can talk to one other person in the room while making colcannon, but two old biddies chattering away might be distracting).

Irish Stew

Irish stew always goes down well because there are at least some parts of it that you can eat. For example, if the meat is too hard, the potatoes may be a nice mushiness, or if the carrots are still raw, the watery part can serve as a soup. Furthermore, Irish stew is accommodating to vegetarians, as it is a simple matter to push the meat parts over to one side of the plate.

That pot doesn't look too clean.

Ingredients:

- A load of beef or lamb, probably the weight of a small dog or a heavy brick;
- 2 tbsp plain flour;
- 1kg potatoes, peeled and cut into quarters;
- 120g onions;
- 100g leeks;
- 180g carrots;
- 750 mls beef stock;
- A few cabbage leaves cut up and thrown in at the last minute;
- Ah, sure, throw in a few sausages as well.

Method:

1. Cut the meat into chunks and fry with butter in a large pot.
2. Add the stock and simmer for 1.5 hours.
3. Go and change the duvet covers.
4. Throw in the sliced onions and leeks and leave to cook for a further 20 minutes.
5. Boil the potatoes in a separate pot and add to stew.
6. I'm sure I've forgotten to include some of the ingredients in the list above, so just add them as well at some stage. Listen, it's always going to taste the same anyway.

Roast Chicken

The main method of cooking a roast chicken is cremation, in honor of Our Lord's death or what have you. If the chicken comes out with any moisture in it, it contains poison.

To gauge the correct length of time that the bird should be in the oven, pick a time and then double it. When the skin comes off in one go, like a sheet of paper, it's done.

The Fires in Hell Don't Burn This Long

Ingredients:

- Whole chicken;
- Real buttery butter;
- Extra-large roasting pan that fits into oven when you tilt it slightly and scrape the sides as you force it in.

Method:

1. Remove plastic wrapper from chicken and place bird on roasting pan.
2. Remember something about giblets.
3. Go to 10 o'clock Mass.
4. Cousin Annie by marriage is in the fifth row and says the giblets have to be removed by hand. She sold quiches to the local Spar before she was crippled with arthritis, so she knows what she's talking about.
5. Rush home to find chicken still in the kitchen.
6. Wash hands with too much diligence, then hold the top of chicken and place other hand in chicken's backside (or is that the head area?).
7. Say "Jesus" a few times and find nothing. Feel a bit dirty. Wonder if this particular chicken has any giblets. Continue with preparation, giblets or no.
8. With a knife, spread butter on top of chicken. Place knife in sink and remind oneself to clean it later.
9. Place chicken, on roasting pan, into oven, preheated for a few minutes to what feels about 100 degrees when you open the door. Turn oven up to around 180 degrees.
10. Leave to roast until guests arrive, three hours later. Marvel at how well it turns out.

Coddle

No one in Ireland heard of coddle until 1998, when the country got a bit of money and Dublin restaurants had to invent traditional Irish recipes for the tourists who were flocking over. They decided to throw a few burnt sausages into a pot of leftovers.

They say the word 'coddle' has its origins in a verb meaning 'to boil gently,' and even further back, from the Latin word 'caudle,' a warm drink for sick people. So in an ironic sort of way, coddle may be both the cause and the cure.

Some commentators suggest that this stew dish had its origins during the Irish famine, which is ridiculous as everyone knows Irish people had only grass and fish to eat back them. If there is a grass and fish coddle, however, they may be correct.

Restaurant Coddle...

...or frankfurters in water, as we called it at home.

Ingredients:

- A huge metal pot commonly used to throw hot water over the car in snowy weather;
- High-fat uncooked sausages from big fat pigs;
- A pack of Denny rashers;
- A handful of potatoes, peeled and with only one or two eyes left in;
- Two white onions;
- Seasoning: salt (pepper didn't enter the Irish consciousness until the 1980s, and any other spices are only used by people who are showing off);
- Herbs: anything green, and let's call it parsley.

Method:

1. Peel one onion, then decide that's enough for now as eyes badly affected.
2. Place onion peelings and all other ingredients into large pot.
3. Look for matching lid, improvise with smaller lid balanced on side of pot, retrieving it whenever it slides into stew.
4. Leave to simmer for half a day, to ensure the potatoes are done.
5. Remove lid and take one look. Step away from pot with an involuntary wincing expression.
6. Rescue potatoes to use again, but that's about it. There is boiled pig meat in there, after all, and that's just rotten.

Read This...

One explanation for Ireland's dreadful cuisine is the remarkable **fecundity** of its inhabitants. Rome told us that condoms were the devil's hat, and every Irish person took the words of an old virgin in a frock very seriously.

Contraceptives that were in any way effective were outlawed until 1980, and even for a few years after that, you had to have a prescription from a doctor to get them.

The know-it-alls in Rome allowed a woman to listen to her body signals to determine whether she was fertile when performing her marital duty, a method that is as helpful as steering a boat into the coast without the aid of a lighthouse, eyes, or a boat. When you have ten children, selecting 20 different varieties of tomato for one dish, à la some celebrity chefs, does not seem that important.

Lasagna

Lasagna was discovered by Irish mothers in the late 1970s, when they felt like being a bit more uppity in the kitchen. It helped that dried sheets of pasta appeared in shops, along with jars of the necessary cooking sauces and the cheesy creamy component. Having now been in Ireland for so long, Lasagna is practically Irish.

The dish was whipped out when the fancier guests were calling round, especially potential in-laws. Irish mothers often used the right amount of beef mince demanded by the recipe, because the guests could be responsible for finally taking their 40-year-old son or daughter off their hands. Lasagna is always served with straight or crinkly chips.

Screaming with Flavor

Ingredients:

- 500g minced beef;
- Packet of Lasagna pasta sheets;
- Jar of creamy Lasagna sauce;
- Jar of tomato sauce for Lasagna;
- Handfuls of grated cheddar.

Method:

1. Fry the mince in the pan for what seems like ages, turning bits over here and there to take the red look off.
2. Stir the jar of tomato sauce into the beef and continue to fry and stir like there's no tomorrow.
3. Place half of this fried mixture into the bottom of a flat oven-proof dish, preferably a rectangular one otherwise there may be trouble ahead.
4. Arrange Lasagna sheets on top, breaking them up where necessary and working with architectural skill to get them to cover the mince mixture entirely.
5. Spread what you believe is half of the jar of creamy Lasagna sauce on top of the pasta layer.
6. Spread the rest of the mince mixture on top of that one, then cover with another layer of pasta.
7. Begin to empty the rest of the creamy sauce on top of the pasta layer, but realize that you used far more than half the last time, so spread in a Loaves-and-Fishes kind of way and hope for the best.
8. Place in preheated oven at 180 degrees or else go mad and try 200 degrees, for half an hour. Stay next to the oven door all that time, watching. It would be

nice to have the extra space in the vacated bedroom.
9. Serve with chips.

Vegetarian Lasagna

Ingredients:

- See previous recipe;
- Copy word for word.

Method:

1. See previous recipe;
2. Copy word for word;
3. Serve with chips;
4. Say nothing.

Still Screaming with Flavor

Boxty

Boxty is a food traditionally prepared up in the mad northern counties, so like coddle, no one had ever heard of it in the rest of Ireland until the country went yuppie in the 1990s.

Restaurants began serving it as if their grandmother had given them a secret recipe while they were children sitting on her bony knee by the open hearth. People who 'do' recipes for a living describe it as being akin to a potato pancake.

That doesn't look half bad, maybe those Northerners aren't that crazy after all.

Ingredients:

- One bowl of yesterday's leftover cold, cooked potatoes (this is already a challenge as potatoes are rarely ever left behind in an Irish household);
- The same amount of raw potatoes, which is doable;
- One bowl of flour;
- One teaspoon of good old baking powder from the back of the shelf;
- Pinch salt;
- Enough milk and melted butter to bind to a dough.

Method:

1. Mix the leftover spuds and the raw ones in a large bowl. When it doesn't work so well, grate the individual raw spuds back into the bowl and try again.
2. In a separate bowl, mix together the flour, salt, baking powder, milk and melted butter until it becomes like dough.
3. Knead the dough on a floured board until you can start to see something happening. Seemingly, you're aiming for something that you can fry to look like a pancake, but good luck with that.
4. Divide the dough into sections and fry on a hot griddle, if you're living in the 1890s, or on an oiled pan. You should end up with something that looks like a pancake. If you don't, you're not a great cook.

Roast Beef Dinner

Roast beef with all the trimmings: potatoes slow roasted in goose fat, honey glazed melt-in-the-mouth baby carrots, soft garden peas, Yorkshire puddings with home-made succulent gravy.

Undoubtedly an 'Anglo-Irish' dish, don't even think about making it. The best option is to head over to a neighbor's house at the appropriate time.

Roast Beef Dinner

Ingredients:

A potted chrysanthemum.

Method:

1. Turn up at the house of your friendly Anglo-Irish neighbor at approximately 5 o'clock on Sunday evening (they eat late). Make up a story about thinking how great the plant would look in their garden, and you have an 18% chance of being invited in for dinner.
2. Leave after the meal and before they start talking fancy.

Difficulty level: Unknown (result depends on who the neighbor is).

Black Pudding

Foreigners, don't be fooled. This is not some kind of delightful chocolate dessert, nor some Bavarian sponge cake topped with sprinkles. Despite the word 'pudding' in the title, this is actually a type of sausage made from the blood of a pig.

Onions, pork fat, fillers such as oatmeal or barley, and various flavorings are added to blood that is drained from a live animal. Most countries have some form of black pudding, or blood sausage, because it was a handy way of making food without killing the livestock.

White pudding contains minced liver instead of blood. Still sounds like muck, but tasty enough.

Ingredients:

- 4 cups fresh pig's blood;
- 200g pinhead oatmeal;
- 200g pork fat, finely chopped;
- 1 onion, finely chopped;
- 1 cup milk;
- 2 tsp black pepper;
- 1 tsp allspice.

Method:

1. Kill a pig and drain its blood.
2. Alternatively, sneak up on a live pig and drain its blood.
3. Alternatively, buy four cups of freshly drained pig's blood from the butcher.
4. Stir the salt into the blood and pray to the Holy Lord Mary Mother of Jesus that it's not a black mass you've started to celebrate and will the devil come in the window now?
5. Boil approx. half a liter of water and add the oatmeal to it, then simmer for 15 minutes.
6. Pour the blood through a sieve into a large bowl to remove any lumps, oh holy god that sounds disgusting.
7. Stir in the fat, onion, milk, pepper, allspice and pinch of salt. Add the oatmeal and combine. Spread the mixture between two greased and lined loaf pans, cover with tin foil, and bake for one hour at 170 degrees.

8. Allow to cool completely.
9. When serving, best off to fry it again, just in case.
10. Go to confession on Friday evening and ask the priest whether he should perform an exorcism. Feel better when he says you probably have 'generalized anxiety disorder' and try not to worry about letting **an Fear Dubh** in the door.

Sundries

If everyday meals in Ireland, such as lunch and dinner, may be described as 'can't-be-arsed' cuisine, then the dishes that fall under Sundries are the 'definitely-can't-be-fecking-arsed' cuisine. These are the snacks and the sides that you create when you haven't the time, the patience, or the inclination to work out if what you are eating is actually edible or not.

Sugary Toast

Sugary Toast

There's a reason why Scandinavia is known as the **Spock of Europe** (I'm not sure it is). For them, life is about logical decisions made for the good of the many, particularly when it comes to their health and traffic management systems.

It is therefore bizarre that in Scandinavia, you can buy bars of chocolate that are specifically created for spreading on bread for breakfast. This custom seems to transcend age and class boundaries, so that the richest and the poorest, youngest and oldest, can be found eating what is effectively a bar of chocolate for breakfast. And nobody mentions that what they are eating is a bar of chocolate for breakfast.

The only difference between these products, **Palaeg Chokolade**, and normal chocolate is that they come in thin slices for easier spreading. You can get them in plain or milk chocolate, and you can lather them on standard white bread or brown bread, or even the Scandinavian staple, rye bread, which they call bread but which is actually a type of bark.

But don't scoff at this disgustingness, for the Irish are worse: we have **sugary toast**, a treat for little ones when I was growing up. The attraction of sugary toast must be the idea of it, rather than its taste or grainy texture, which is like eating some kind of bready glass feathers.

Ingredients:

- Heart-stopping white bread slices;
- Heart-destroying full-fat buttery butter;
- Heart-leveling white sugar, probably a full kilo.

Method:

1. Spread liberal amounts of butter on slices of white bread.
2. Sprinkle a copious amount of white sugar on top, covering every inch, especially the tough-to-chew crust.
3. Toast until the sugar just starts to bubble and the smell of caramelization sticks to your new kitchen units.

Tip: It's best to use a flat grill for this, such as you'd find in your oven, as an upright toaster might bring challenges.

Irish Scones

Irish scones sound fantastic, particularly if the recipes are accompanied by pictures of butter-filled creations or ladles of strawberry jam and whipped cream. The reality is, however, very different, as scones that are baking have a tendency to ignore the rules of physics and space-time and to come out with the characteristics of a typical Irish convict in 19th-century Australia: hard as nails.

Ingredients:

- 450g self-raising flour;
- Pinch baking powder;
- Pinch salt;
- 50g caster sugar;
- 110g butter;
- 1 egg;
- 50ml double cream;
- 200ml milk;
- 1 beaten egg to glaze.
-

Method:

1. Sift the flour, baking powder and salt into a bowl and stir in the sugar. Rub the butter in until it all looks like breadcrumbs.
2. Add the egg, cream and enough milk to blend into a soft dough.
3. Turn the ball onto a floured board and give it a nice little slap and roll with a rolling pin until 1-2 inches thick.
4. Cut out circles with a round cutter or a fancy wavy cutter and transfer to a greased baking tray.
5. Brush the tops with the egg glaze.
6. Bake in an oven preheated to the magical 180 degrees for 15 to 20 minutes.

Tip: You can add raisins or cinnamon but it's a bit of a waste because they're going to be too hard to eat anyway.

Egg in a Cup

The main question that surrounds this Irish delicacy is existential: why bother?

Isn't it just the same as boiling an egg and mixing it with a lot of butter? Maybe there was something magical about an egg in a cup in a pot on a stove at 6 o'clock in the evening when the news was on.

The main advantages of egg in a cup are that it's quick and easy, but it also gets the protein into you.

Egg in a Cup

Ingredients:

- An egg;
- Two tablespoons of butter;
- A cup and a pot of boiling water.

Method:

1. Stand the cup in the pot of boiling water and crack the egg into it.
2. Stir the egg as it begins to cook; this may take several minutes.
3. Add the butter and mix well.
4. Serve to your child with a spoon and some story about the Pharaohs of Egypt eating exactly the same thing.

Difficulty level: Easy (you can watch telly at the same time).

See This...

Peig Sayers, a woman who was only ever happy when she was falling off a cliff.

Crisp Sandwich

The potato arrived in Ireland around the year 1600, and shortly afterward it was discovered that it could be turned into the exquisite regional delicacy known as the crisp sandwich.

Savory and dessert at the same time, portable yet filling, the crisp sandwich has been an icon to young and old alike. Unfortunately, it is going out of fashion nowadays, with health enthusiasts promoting water as a snack instead.

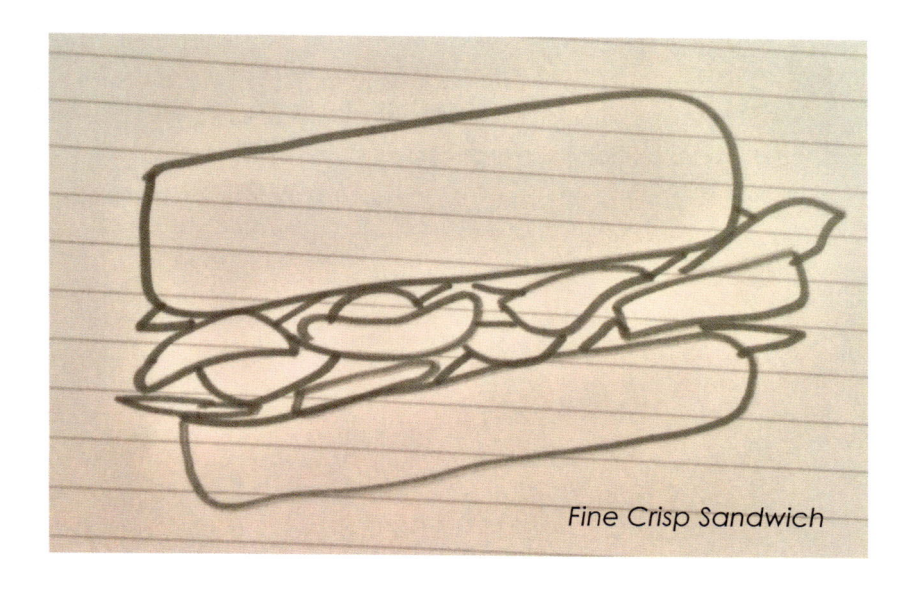

Fine Crisp Sandwich

There are no crisp sandwich photographs on the stock image sites, which is bizarre, so this will have to do.

Ingredients:

- Four slices of bread, as fresh as the day they were baked, give or take a day;
- A bag of either cheese and onion or salt and vinegar crisps, newly opened.
- A small amount of butter.

Method:

1. Spread a very thin layer of butter on one side of each of the slices of bread, choosing whichever side is more amenable at the time. The butter must be thin as possible as it serves merely as an anchor between the crisps and the bread.
2. Pour a generous amount of crisps onto the buttered side of one slice of bread.
3. Top with another slice the bread, the buttered side facing inward.
4. Press down on the three layers until you are reasonably satisfied that the crisps will not fall out.

Summer Salad (aka Winter Salad)

Salads tend to be served in Ireland during the summer months, prepared optimistically when the sun has been out for two hours and is surely going to stay out for the next three months. The main function of salads in Ireland is as decoration.

Not much happening here.

Ingredients:

- A head of leafy lettuce;
- Two tomatoes, sliced;
- Two very hard-boiled eggs;
- Two slices of packet ham;
- Cheddar cheese;
- A handful of chopped scallions (spring onions to the civilized world).

Method:

1. Wash the lettuce in order to remove most of the tiny flies. Cut the leaves off whole and place them, still wet, at the base of a large bowl.
2. Add the scallions, plus slices of the tomatoes.
3. Break up the ham into smaller pieces and add to bowl.
4. Grate the cheese into the bowl.
5. Cut the boiled eggs into halves, and place the halves on top as if there are more lurking underneath.
6. If adventurous, add slices of beetroot from a jar, turning the entire contents of the bowl a purple-red color.
7. If a dressing is required, Irish legislation mandates that it must be mayonnaise. Fancy dressings are an unnecessary turbulence.

Variations: Winter Salad, Spring Salad, Autumn Salad
Ingredients and Method: Same as above.

Soda Bread

Soda bread is a traditional Irish creation, mainly because yeast, used for normal-bread making, was generally associated with something found growing on bodies. And not in the nether regions, either, because every Irish person is an immaculate conception. Packets of yeast were not used by Irish mothers because you had to have dark powers to get yeast and hot water to work. If you knew an Anglo-Irish individual, they could do it for you.

Therefore, soda bread, with its modest ingredient list of flour, salt, buttermilk, and a rusted tin of sodium bicarbonate, was achievable. The preparation became even easier in the late 1990s, when Odlums introduced its ready-made packets of the dried ingredients for soda bread. You simply added milk to the mix, but this step meant you could claim you made the entire thing by hand. If you want to be all snooty, here's the genuine handmade version:

Ingredients:

- A carton of buttermilk, as if you have one;
- A half bowl of flour, sifted;
- Pinch of salt;
- Sodium bicarbonate.

Method:

1. Add salt to sifted flour, then add good swig of buttermilk to flour mix.
2. Retrieve rusty tin of sodium bicarbonate from back of press, prize open with teaspoon, screwdriver, or the cold, dead hands of a lodger. Place two heaped teaspoons of bicarbonate into bowl.
3. Give everything a good mix, then place the goop in round, buttered tin. Using a knife, cut the sign of the cross into the bread, for the sake of the baby Jesus on the cross.
4. Put in oven, at the exact temperature required, until it starts to turn brown, then open oven door every ten minutes after that to check on progress. Miraculously, remember to take the bread out just before it starts to go black around the edges. Thank the baby Jesus for the burnt smell in the kitchen that reminded you that you had something in the oven.
5. Cut the soda bread using some effort with blunt knife, spread with butter or jam.
6. Remind oneself to buy a white sliced pan before the shops close at 8 pm.

Desserts

If all else fails, the Dairy Milk is always in the press.

Sherry Trifle

This ancient creation was used by the Romans as missiles in their trebuchets. In Ireland, it was liberally fed to adults and children alike, despite whatever volume of alcohol the cook had a mind to put in.

The cream and custard part of this concoction always eaten, then regretted afterwards as the sugar overdose kicked in. The jelly and sponge layer was left on the plate, unless some of the cream and custard could be sacrificed and mixed into the jelly mess to offset the taste.

Sickly sweet and generously sherried – a taste explosion in the most dangerous sense of the phrase.

Oh God, Aunty Maura, you've made two of them. Aren't you great?

Ingredients:

- Packet of sponge fingers that have been sitting in the window of the local shop for three years and would now make a worthwhile addition to the foundation of a house;
- Tin fruit cocktail, see source above;
- Sherry, best brand if son's mother-in-law is calling round, worst if anyone else;
- Packet of Chiver's strawberry jelly, raspberry if cook is the adventurous type;
- Tin powdered custard;
- Single cream (double is slightly dearer).

Method:

1. Invite all the oul ones round.
2. Dissolve jelly in an unmeasured volume of water, pouring out a bit until it looks ok.
3. Try to fit sponge fingers into bottom of round-bottomed bowl.
4. Pour a small slug of sherry on top.
5. Pour the jelly mixture over the sponges.
6. Slide the contents of the fruit cocktail tin out and into the bowl, then stare it at to see how many red cherries were in the tin (2 on a good day).
7. Sit down with the oul ones, who are very interested in the brand of sherry. Discuss how the absent Florrie snored every night at last year's trip to Lourdes. Insist on not getting Florrie as room companion this year.
8. Mix spoonfuls of custard powder with boiled milk,

using teaspoon used to open tin. Unable to remove lumps, despite vigorous stirring. Pour custard over jelly and sponge mixture.
9. Sit down with the ladies to taste the now-poured-out sherry.
10. Leap out of seat after remembering to whisk single cream. Half-whisk it then spoon semi-thickened, watery cream over top of trifle. On the top, add a few colored sprinkles that someone has in their bag.
11. Place in middle shelf of fridge, lopsidedly, one half balanced on egg carton.
12. Open freezer compartment and take out Arctic Roll, for emergency use.

Difficulty level: Fairly Damn Hard, especially given the result.

Agree With This...

Uniquely Irish

People on the continent can spend four hours cooking a meal, then another four sitting around the table eating and talking about the food they're eating. Irish people don't do that. Left in a room full of continentals, we'll always be the first to finish our plates. The foreign cultures don't even look down their noses at us for not having the same sense of gourmanderie, because there's no Irish cuisine for them to analyze and compare themselves to. Them with their food going cold in front of them.

That's not to say that Irish people don't enjoy Sunday dinner around the ma's with the whole family as much as any other nationality, and even more so. The day begins with the eating, which takes less than an hour, and then on to higher things. This may be the stereotypical rivers of booze, or the cut-throat board games, cards or wonky charades, or simply just sitting round on whatever chairs come to hand, lost in lively chat.

The Irish are not renowned for their winning food, but they are the masters of the craic. Better still, no one has to spend hours in the kitchen to create an evening of banter, laughs, and fun that will live on in the memory forever. Lukewarm cocktail sausages are just fine in the early hours.

Queen Cakes/Fairy Cakes

The name of these little terrors is interchangeable in Ireland, both phrases meaning tiny dirt-dry sponge cakes, sitting in fairy cake cases that are either plain white or have a few colored spots on them for fanciness.

In the good old days, these buns made do without decoration, but in the 1970s, the discovery in Ireland of icing sugar made them just about palatable. Vanilla-tasting sponge may have been fine on its own, but there was always too much baking powder added, so the taste was that of tongue-sticking vanilla baking powder.

Queen cakes / Fairy cakes are a nonsense because you go to so much time and expense to find the bun cases in the shop, and they look as if they hold so much promise. Then you fill them with plain sponge, which really should only ever be used as a base in larger, more glamourous delicacies. We've been fooled all these years.

Ingredients:

- 6 tablespoons self-raising flour;
- 2 tablespoons baking powder (even though self-raising flour is already being used, you want that tasty baking powder 'hit' or else what's the point?);
- 4 tablespoons sugar;
- 4 tablespoons butter or margarine;
- 2 eggs.

Method:

1. Sift flour and baking powder into a bowl, then throw in all other ingredients and stir like you're touched. If mixture is too stiff, add whatever liquid is to hand.
2. Turn oven on to the magical 180 degrees, a temperature that seems to cook most things.
3. Open plastic paper-case container and start taking out individual cases. Get very agitated after lifting out two or three at a time, and fiddle around to try and separate them. Eventually place single paper cases in holes of a metal bun tin.
4. Pop in middle of oven for about 20 minutes, or however long it takes to place old towel around shoulders and put Nice and Easy Light Golden Brown hair dye in hair.
5. Remove very, very brown buns from oven, then leave to cool on kitchen unit while you wash the dye out.
6. To make up icing sugar: forget about sifting as icing sugar breaks down in small amounts of water

anyway. Empty half contents icing sugar package into bowl. Place bowl under sink tap and add far too much water. After looking on in horror as the icing sugar melts away to nothing and the mixture remains as watery as if it had itself come out of the tap, empty rest of icing sugar bag into mixture.

7. Thank the Lord's holy high heavenly saints when the mixture starts to thicken, then get a sinking feeling when it stirs into water again.
8. Pour spoonfuls of the watery icing over the cool buns, and wondrously run out of icing sugar before the last few are covered. Daub a spoon of jam on top of those ones and no one's the wiser.
9. Silvery balls hide a multitude of ills, so retrieve a plastic container full of them from the cupboard and sprinkle liberally on top of cakes.
10. Watch impotently as the balls start to slide off the cake with the movement of the runny icing.
11. Remember to buy a lottery ticket tonight.

Barmbrack

The meaning of Barmbrack comes from the Irish *báirín breac,* or speckled loaf. When you have the word 'loaf' as part of a dessert name, it never turns out well.

The exciting thing about the barmbrack is that it's associated with Halloween, which is always a good time for teenagers to go drinking around bonfires, meaning their parents can get a break from them. Furthermore, on the night of Halloween the door between Hell and Earth is opened, which is always great fun.

Barmbrack, which the photographer in this instance thought would look appetizing placed on a toilet seat.

Ingredients:

- 200g plain flour;
- 2 teaspoons of baking powder;
- 350g packet of fruit mix;
  250 mls cold tea;
- 50 mls of whiskey;
  125g light brown sugar;
- 1 large egg;
- 2 teaspoons mixed spice.

Method:

1. Preheat the oven to 170 degrees and butter up a good sized loaf tin.
2. Sieve and combine the flour, baking powder, sugar, and spice, then break an egg in and stir.
3. Add enough of the liquid to achieve a wet dough.
4. Add the fruit to the bowl.
5. Get the dough into the loaf tin by pouring or spooning, and place in the oven for an hour.
6. It should be grand, if not to eat, then to feed to the birds when the winter comes.

> I hope you haven't baked it yet because at step four, it's traditional to add a ring to the mixture. Whoever gets the slice with the ring will marry within a year. You can also add a rag (for poverty), a pea (no wedding for you this year), a stick (arguments or a bad marriage), a coin (wealth), and a Mars bar (the brack turned out badly).

*Why would you want these,
when you can have this...*

Christmas Pudding

Irish people stopped eating this in the mid-1990s when they finally admitted that it tasted like kack. They continued to make it, however, as gifts for unexpected visitors and unloved ones. The remarkable thing about the Christmas pudding is that even though there are a myriad variations for making it, they all taste the bloody same in the end.

A delightful Christmas pudding (which is itself puking).

Ingredients:

- 600g currants/raisins/sultanas, in any combination as Irish people lack the gene to tell these mummified fruits apart;
- Mug of butter;
- Mug of brown sugar;
- 4 eggs;
- 200g breadcrumbs, made from stale bread, thankfully;
- Tub of candied peel;
- 1 teaspoon ground mixed spice, to cover smell of candied peel;
- Grated rind of 1 orange and 1 lemon;
- Guinness and Brandy.
- Andrew's Liver Salts.

Method:

1. Mix all the dry ingredients together.
2. Beat the eggs and add them to the dry mixture.
3. Add enough Guinness to obtain a – let's face it – poo-like consistency.
4. Grease a pudding bowl and pour the mixture into it. Cover the top of bowl with greaseproof paper, tying string around the top to make sure it doesn't fly off.
5. I'd love to tell you to stick it in the oven for half an hour, but you actually have to place it in a pot of boiling water that reaches two-thirds up the bowl. Simmer this for a whopping eight to ten hours, adding more water when the level drops low.

6. After the allotted time, take out the pudding and pour some brandy over it. Then wrap it in new greaseproof paper, then in foil, and leave for weeks and weeks. A lot of the old ladies say that if you see a bit of mould growing on the pudding, just slice it off and douse in a little brandy again. This is a total health hazard, I'm sure of it.
7. Serve with cream of brandy butter, which is 4 tablespoons each of butter, brandy, and icing sugar mixed together. I'd like to say all of this tastes even better than it sounds, but ethics forbids me.

Difficulty level: Ridiculously Hard (and certainly not worth it).

Think About This...

Irish Mammies are Unique

And it's not just the sherry that's to blame for that...

The Skills of Irish Mammies

- Irish mothers can dip their hands into a pot of boiling ham to retrieve the plastic covering they forgot to take off. They will not even be aware that the water is in any way hot, and their hand will come out unaffected.
- Similarly, Irish mothers can carry hot plates over to the table with their bare hands, and without wincing.
- It is a famous stereotype, but it is true: Irish mothers will ask you repeatedly if you are hungry or you want seconds. They will always hear an affirmative reply, whether or not it was given. Irish fathers will always ask if you want another Guinness, as sociability is the only way the other half will let them have another one.
- Irish mothers will always have pre-buttered the bread slices or rolls that are sitting on the table.
- Don't look too closely at the cutlery, given that dishwashers didn't really start coming into Ireland until 1991.
- Irish mothers do not follow recipes that are written down, nor do they often use weighing scales. They really should, in both instances.

Christmas Cake

Christmas cake is the dry equivalent of the thick, wet, stodgy Christmas pudding. The ingredients are practically the same, but this seems to be some kind of open secret that no one talks about.

What usually happens at Christmas is that the Christmas cake is brought out, divided, and eaten, then the Christmas pudding is taken out to eat. No one mentions that they're almost the same cake.

Icing and bits of a tree can't hide what's inside.

Ingredients:

- 275g plain flour;
- 225g sugar;
- 225g butter or margarine;
- 4 eggs;
- 600g of currants/raisins/sultanas or what have you;
- Tub candied peel;
- Grated rind and juice of 1 orange;
- 100g ground almonds, to differentiate the cake from Christmas pudding, hurrah;
- Napkins to conceal the leftovers.

Method:

1. Preheat oven to 150°C/300°F/ Gas 2. Line and grease your round cake tin. Apologize to both tin and oven.
2. Place sugar and margarine/butter into mixing bowl and beat until creamy. Gradually add the eggs, trying to have patience to beat well after each addition. Pick out stray hairs.
3. Stir in the almonds, orange rind and juice, then stir in the flour.
4. Mix in the dried fruit and peel.
5. Pour mixture into the tin, pop in the oven, and bake for roughly 3 hours, though really God only knows.
6. If the cake's done, a sharp knife stuck into the middle of it will come out without any wet mixture

7. trying to make its escape. Otherwise, stick the cake back in the oven and check with a knife every 15 minutes until the top of the cake has been stabbed as much as Caesar.
8. Allow to cool in tin and store in a cool dry place until you're ready to pretend it's a wonderful creation by covering it in marzipan and fancy icing decorations.

I'm grand, thank you

And if, during the summer, you should need a doorstop.

Difficulty level: Divorce Territory (*"why are you making that horrible thing again?"*)

Camouflaging the Cake:

Spread apricot jam around the entire cake so that the marzipan will stick to it and not just flap off to the sides. Take a huge block of marzipan and heat it in the microwave for about 30 seconds. Then roll it out and press it down gently onto the cake, brushing out air pockets that seem to be everywhere. Most Irish mothers then brush the marzipan layer with brandy or whiskey, but water is just as effective as all this step does is moisten the marzipan to stick to the fondant layers. Those naughty mothers!

As for decorations, anything goes, once it's not minimalist. When used together, holly, a Santa, an igloo, a snowman, a reindeer, penguins, the little baby Jesus, and a small pond are good starting points, after which you can add your own little touches.

Neapolitan Ice Cream Wafers

At the end of dinner, we would all gather around the Superser heater and enjoy our Neapolitan ice-cream wafers. Two cardboards of air holding together a slice of that chocolate, vanilla, and strawberry ice cream that was stuck at the back of the fridge freezer since last year.

We would look at each other and our ice cream, and we would enjoy the company, enhanced by the colorful layers of cold delight in our hands. It lasted about seven minutes and then we went back to beating the heads off each other, but at least our Irish Mammy had those seven minutes of peace.

The Drink

Every good Irish meal is accompanied by a choice of drinks from a range whose sugar, alcohol or caffeine level is sufficient to overcome the blandness of the food. These beverages can be mixed and matched, taken on their own or combined with every other damn thing on the list:

Guinness: Brewed in Ireland since 1759, Guinness is now available in more than 160 countries, so no matter where you are, you're always there. Suitable for every occasion, from happy (christenings and weddings) to sad (wakes and family get-togethers).

Tea/Coffee: Tea is the reason for Ireland's historically low divorce rate. Having to drink six cups a day gives couples something to talk about and, more importantly, something to do, especially when the years have passed, all the kids have grown up, and there's shite all else happening.

Coffee is more of a modern introduction, but we have taken to it vehemently and even produced the best coffee experience in the world, the Irish coffee. Have a look at our recipes in the coming pages, or else go on Facebook and see what your friends are up to.

A Nice Cup of Tea, Just a Half for Me

Irish men and women over a certain age (60 nowadays) and Holy Joes of any age never drink more than a half cup of tea at any sitting. It's a way of getting in as many cups in during the day without dying of caffeine poisoning.

Reports suggest that herbal teas and caffeine-free beverages are still illegal in Ireland.

Ingredients:

- Two tea bags;
- A kettle of boiling water, boiled once and once only;
- Enough sugar to keep the plantations busy;
- Full-fat milk.

Method:

1. Fill a teapot with boiling water from a kettle and set aside for the pot to warm up.
2. Meanwhile, place the sugar, milk and box of tea on the kitchen unit.
3. If alone, look out of the window for signs of activity among the neighbors and mentally record what they are up to. If in company, discuss the weather as an opener, then one's minor ailments, then mutually distrusted acquaintances.
4. Decant the water in the teapot into the sink, then place teabags in teapot and fill pot with water from the kettle.
5. Using a dessert spoon, squeeze the teabags against the side of pot.
6. Replace lid and leave to brew for a few minutes.
7. Pour tea into cups, then add three teaspoons of sugar to each, and enough milk to achieve a lukewarm temperature.
8. Decant half of the tea mixture from the cups into the sink and drink the rest.

Coffee Made on Milk

Coffee made with hot full-fat milk and lots of sugar was an evening treat in my childhood home, and the rest of the world had to catch up a few years later with the Latte.

There was no frothiness back then, nor cinnamon or any of the other additions that might ruin milky coffee. Your own eight-year-old will like one today, again at around 7 o'clock at night. Good luck.

You probably know what a cup of coffee looks like, so here's a nice Irish scene instead.

Irish Coffee

Enormously tasty, the Irish coffee is more of a milkshake than an alcoholic beverage. Invented by Limerick man Joseph Sheridan in 1942, the drink consists of coffee, whiskey, brown sugar and whipped cream.

Irish coffees appeal to all ages, especially the seniors who don't like other people to know that they're drinking anything alcoholic at all, so feel fine about ordering three in a row. After that, they feel very fine indeed.

Difficulty level: Hopelessly Tough, always get a barman with grey or no hair to make one for you.

Stay Away From This…

Poitín

Poitín

This beverage, distilled from potatoes or barley, was outlawed in Ireland from 1661 to 1989, and with good reason – a typical example could reach 95 percent alcohol by volume. The illegality didn't stop the Irish, though, and we continued to make it at home, leading to outbreaks of alcohol poisoning, blindness, and happy days.

Minerals

Miwadi: Sugar-laden fruit cordial for the little scuts on their birthday.

TK Red Lemonade: Confined to Ireland, TK red lemonade was like normal lemonade except for the addition of artificial colors and sweeteners to give you a buzz in the days before Red Bull.

Flat Cola: Passed off as Real Coke by generations of mothers, flat cola was a bittersweet treat at the beach. Thirsty after standing at the edge of the ice-cold sea for an hour or being poked by the spikey grass while tumbling down the sand dunes, you looked forward to an ice cold coke that scratched your throat as you excitedly drank it. Instead, you would get a melamine cup full of warm, flat cola. And you'd love it.

Irish Whiskey

The word 'whiskey' comes from *uisce beatha,* the Irish phrase for 'water of life.' In reality, it should come from 'holy God, that burns the throat, but now I'm set up for the day.'

Irish whiskey is made from a blend of malted and unmalted barley, whereas Scotch whiskey (or 'whisky,' as they spell it) is made from only malted barley. While the Scotch form is dried over peat smoke, giving it a smoky flavor, Irish whiskey is made from kiln-dried barley, so it tastes more like the grain itself.

Furthermore, Scotch whisky is distilled twice, whereas the Irish go one step more and distil it three times, resulting in a smoother drink with a higher alcohol content, boyo.

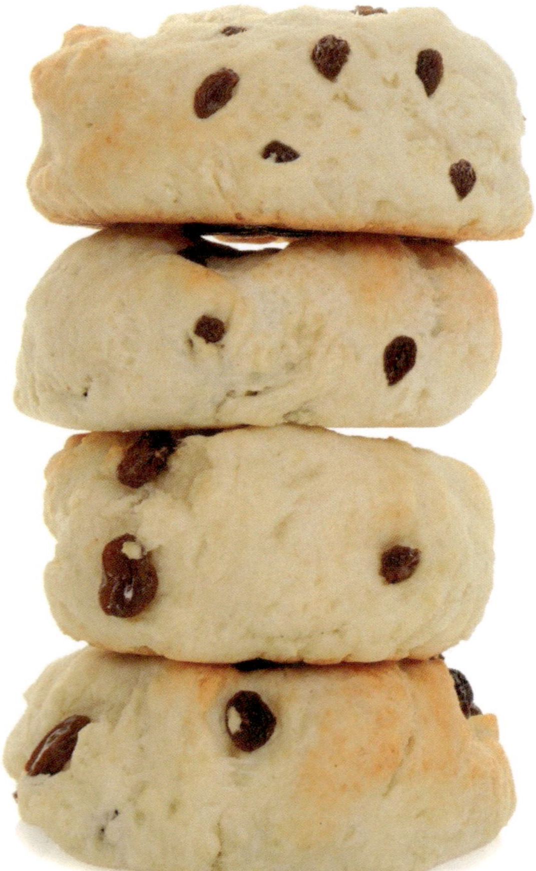

Your Notes

Write your own notes and favorite Irish recipes in this box:

Printed in Great Britain
by Amazon